I0749448

Contents

NATIONAL TREE
CALABASH
CRESCENTIA CUJETE

The Calabash Tree – St. Lucia's National Tree

"A Loving Tree"

In St. Lucia the Calabash Fruit is used mainly for its outer shell. The pulp is removed from the shell, after this the shell is dried and cured to be fashioned into various articles including, eating utensils, water vessels and other items of personal adornment and household use.

The shell or gourd is not the only part that has use. The pulp or "nana" has medicinal qualities. It can be used for the elimination of gas from the body, among other things.

This truly wonder fruit has a versatility that cannot be counted. Throughout our history, it has graced us, in its many forms. It has form and function, that is as unique as the people of St. Lucia.

Biography

Gandolph St. Clair, poet, playwright, actor and singer was born on April 3rd, 1951, in Vieux Fort. He attended St. Aloysius R.C. Boys' Infant and Primary, Vide Bouteille Gov't School, Choiseul R. C. Boys' Primary and St. May's College, Vigie, St. Lucia. Attended Brixton College and West Norwood Polytechnic in London between 1969-1971, Burnhampthorpe Collegiate of Canada in 1994.

He won a UNESCO bursary in 1979 to attend the Jamaica School of Drama, where he majored in directing, graduating in 1981. His directing credits include his own plays, One Love, 1977's winner of the Howick Ellcock Memorial award for playwrighting; Guess who came to visit the Doctor? in 1978, produced in New Jersey, directed by Irvin Grey and in Port of Spain, directed by Freddie Kisson and performed by The Strolling Players of Trinidad & Tobago; Sir Gawain and the Green Knight by Dennis Scott in 1980; Bins and Tins by Gandolph St. Clair in 1980; Kendel Hippolyte's Drum Maker in 1980; Errol John's Moon on a Rainbow Shawl in 1982; Antigone by Michael Gilkes; Just in Case by Gandolph St. Clair in 2005, Burial at Thebes by Seamus Heaney in 2005; The Harrowing of Benjy by Roderick Walcott in 2010.

The Hustlers, a one act play written by Gandolph St. Clair and Robert Lee has been twice staged in 2003 and 2005, directed by Hayden Forde. Gandolph St. Clair wrote and directed, A Twist In Time, a forty three minute film in 1999, which has been shown locally and in St. Maarten at the Soulaiga Film Festival. Wrote and produced Radio Play "1+1+1" for St. Lucia's 15th independence Anniversary.

As a stage actor, he performed as the first man in One Love in 1977; Asagai in Lorraine Hansberry's Raisin in the Sun; Umberto in Filumena by Eduardo Fillippe; Pindarus and Titinius in William Shakespeare's Julius Caesar; Galileo in Bertolt Bretcht's Galileo; Luigi in Dario Fo's We can't pay, We won't pay; Gonzalo in William Shakespeare's Tempest; Charlie Parker in Unfinished Women directed by Travis Weekes; Augustin in creole version of Derek Walcott's Sea at Dauphin directed by Allan Weekes; Dessalines in stage and film of Derek Walcott's The Haytian Earth in 1984; in 1997, Dr. Bastien in Peter Benchley's film, The Creature, filmed in St. Lucia, starring, Craig T. Nelson and Kim Catrall.

Publications to date are :-Reaching Out- 1982; Urf Song, joint winner of 1983 M&C joint winner of Literary Award; The Patent Man- 1984; The Moon In Daylight-1985; St. Lucia Independence 1979 Short Story "4-2 For True"-1999, Firefall-2005; Just in Case-2007; The Third Umpire-2013. In 1999, Gandolph St. Clair was Director of the National Carnival Development Committee when the celebrations begun with Jam Time in July until the establishment of the Cultural Development Foundation in 2002 where he became Special Events Officer for Carnival.

Participated in Carifesta 1981 in Barbados as part of the Jamaica School of Drama's Graduate Theatre Company as actor in Michael Smith's Foreday Morning and technical (Lights and Sound) operator in Dennis Scott's Dog and Rawle Gibbon's Shepherd. Performed at the 7th Black Book Fair in London and Bradford in 1985. In 2013, Field Producer on "Poetry is an Island" directed by Ida Does documentary on 1992 Nobel Laureate Derek Walcott, premiered in St. Lucia on 22nd January 2014 at Sandals Grande St. Lucia.

In April 2014, The St. Lucia Library Services recognized Gandolph St. Clair for his contribution to St. Lucia's Literary Arts. In 1979, during the 36th Independence Anniversary Celebrations Gandolph St. Clair was awarded the St. Lucia Medal of Merit (Gold) for long and dedicated contribution in the field of Culture and the Arts.In May 2015 he was conferred with honorary membership of the Vide Bouteille Cultural Club for services to the 53 year old voluntary Community Organization.

THE CALABASH TREE

For Richardson Dusauzay
1923 - 2014

It was the last day of October. Heritage. Our Language
Had become an issue, for whatever tongue, my mother
Had, left me since she was not to be there. Her baggage
When she left at five in the morning, in awe of another
Was a suitcase of salted fish with bakes and white rum.
As she dangled her way, up the gangway plank without
Another look at the tears, in my eyes as I stood so numb
That I felt alone in my doom, that I could not even shout.
My father was busy trying to make the clouds go away.
He drove only black cars because the roads were muddy
Whereas the white clouds that rode above the hills turned grey
Every time a death announcement came about a buddy.

I was taken back to the house on Brazil Street, were we
Small unit of four, my granny, her son and pregnant wife
Spoke of names for the new addition to our happy family
So, before I was five, I knew what, I had to go through life.
My own name had people repeating the strange sound
That the more, they mentioned my name, I felt assured
That I was on a special mission, my feet above ground
Sailing on my joystick, with my guardian angel secured.
My plaits were long, my outfit white, my face so very sad
So that, my hands could not touch, the ivory as an outcast
Since being black or white meant being good or bad
Subsequent life must be this journey, where the dice is cast.

As I crossed the Road, to meet Shakespeare for a yarn
The lights went out at the Library, so they closed the door
While I ventured into the arms of a maiden in the barn
With her laughter and chatter, glued to the brown floor.
I was in black and white, she was white, in a dress of white
Her smell, red roses with her tongue oozing with honey
While I stood above her black mine of infinite granite
Confessing to her, that we always need their minted money.
One night after prayers, the earth shook for the first time
I ran into my grandmother's arms as she prayed in creole
There was the sound of the women carrying cans of slime
Along the motionless, dim lit streets littered with people.

When the earth stopped shaking, the naked streets were
Dimly lit with the moon and stars by far the better source
And the reflection of the horses and the whips and the beer
Flowed like the torrents from the hurricanes on their course
And as if that was not enough, the little men from the green
Twin mountains came through the wireless wearing their one
Eyed monocle with bi focal lens satisfying their zealous Queen
With her two colored eyes, one in yellow, another in a red zone.

Their music whatever the mosquitoes sang to their eager ears
Amid the sweat of their brows, the pace of the fondling footsteps
Quiet in prayer and the hum of the clock that counted the years
Memorizing, forever and forever while pumping the vocal biceps.

Poetically, Derek Walcott had written about the fire
Which in 1948, burnt half of the wooden Castries.
There were no deaths but many a token towncrier
Unburdening their distress to the laden breeze.
The St. Aloysius RC Boys' School had been a refuge
The destitute and shocked witnesses of destruction
The rowdy housewives with their sails of subterfuge
The unrepentant Government another investigation.
Opening the windows of the Library, we saw a phoenix
Waltzing to a dirge in the sky past the Eastern High Tower
Above the schoolyard where marbles and water mix
In the flowing fountain of youth immersing there together.

Not only for School but also for life was our motto
The fear in our hearts of falling short in discipline
Could mean, that if you were from Palace or Ghetto
The expectation was not the same, never slot in between.
The discovery of the Castries River was a raw surprise
Yet, as we dared to find its source, we ended in Shit Alley
For on its banks, we built our cricket pitches at Sunrise
By Sunset, we created Lords, after another full century.
Urged by the fish in tins amid thick dark infested waters
The bamboo trees swaying and crackling with ambience
The nagging noise of hammers and saws of squatters
In the wake of Church Bells, the Colonial's conscience.

As the years yawned, the CDC buildings went up high
Was about that same time when Adult Suffrage came.
Forward the women bearers of coal, they could not deny
One voice and a choice, in the shadow hall of fame.
Women contused to be housemaids, banana workers
After the sugar cane vanished in the vapour of alcohol
Barefeet, sweaty, unhygenic bloody clothes of butchers.
They ventured in fashion and religion, the spoils of borbol
Now marching hand in hand, all the way to the Courthouse
Leaving many men running from the long arm of the Street
To a strip to New York, then to meet with Disney's Mickey Mouse
Paying for pleasure, a Wonderland living, out of purple pocket.

The man from the Lodge, came to our open wooden door
As did the Syrian, with his suit case of cloth and clothes
While they both smiled, knowing what they had come for
"Let us not start any negotiating, we have no deal to close".
Then, the white priest, came one afternoon to the School
For he wanted something but there was disagreement.
The Schoolmaster was now the scapegoat and the tool

Knowing that the Church and State equal Government.
While our warm world imploded, my father grew on me
As his world was now feeling the earthquakes I had felt.
He was to be taken from the Pitons that he loved dearly
Whilst I was destined to feel another Schoolmaster's belt.

Reading, Writing and Arithmetic and Schoolmaster Redhead
Who unfortunately for me had the same surname I carried.
He willed that his handwriting I should imitate, vehemently I defied
Thus departing his School following an assembly assault. I hurried
To yet another Schoolmaster with a belt and acid aggression
Voice, smile, cigarettes, whiskey, fits of ritual recognizable recluse
Amid the bustling School driven by his self-determined mission
Challenging our minds to find and store knowledge to use
A photographic memory of scenery, along an early High Street
From whence by bus, we went South to the Morne to Micoud
To Vieux Fort, where my father would take us from the Sun's heat
While the three of us, in silence making our presence a crowd.

When I first met Death, she danced to the howling of the wind-
A young Princess of seven, the electric wire flexed onto her neck.
We placed her body, in a coffin at the Funeral Parlour in a kind
Of disbelief that life was short, a voyage to end in a shipwreck.
The boat would rock and roll, a jiving jewel, justice fit for a crown
To fit Britannia, Queen of the West Indies, Keeper of Fair Helen.
Somehow, we said to the beautiful Pitons, we were going down
And most times whoever left, came up, to wash their dirty linen
To find a job, since Soufriere was the big bountiful bread basket
But the Pitons upstaged the volcano's protective hills, its deep sea
As the grey men sat on their benches and served the fishing net
Beneath the lamps, indented with fireflies, while the waves rolled by.

My mother made me the first black cowboy without a white horse
I had two guns, belt, bullets, black shirt, black pants and waist coat.
This was Carnival, Steelband and I played Davy Crockett off course
As penpals pledged to be friends, fatal floods capsized our longboat.
At St. Mary's, we beat the dust from our books, placed them in bags
Geometry sets and pencil cases together with bread and guava jam.
On the Streets, walking with transistor radios amid paupers in rags
" Doan forget to bring my money for de two can of coke" said Mam.
The Queen of the West Indies came to visit me and the boat rocked
Bajan say "All you trying to kill de Queen" but that was never true
Helen on her high horse rallied her troops although shell shocked
Reined "I'll put a pox on your vox, that's what I will do, a pox on you".

Cloistered Choiseul lit by stars and fireflies under many a street lamp
When at ten, men with long hooks spiked the flaming oil lamps away
While the stark song of crickets and strays, heading for the night camp
Where they ravaged, the fishermen's waste and bait, at the end of day.
There was no water, no electricity, no record player, and no stove.
Upstairs where we lived, my Schoolmaster and I were both convinced

That I would win the first local Scholarship, in my mind a treasure trove
The possibilities of making my grandmother happy, my joy explained.
In the dead of night, the news came, that I had won a Scholarship-
My grandmother was confident, that I had already done so before
Gained admission to St. Mary's, her son, the chaplain of this space ship
Amid the turbulent investigation that followed in settling the score
While the white priest deflated, thus sadly, he threw away the whip.

Ushered into houses, we swore our allegiance to Color and Captains.
We sailed through the rules of competition in Athletics, Cricket, Football
Trained hard at Vigie, conquest of Withers and Wade shield mountains
At the cliff's edge, we healed our wounds impending each other's fall.
The British Soldiers' barracks bore testimony of the legacy of the Rape
Today housing the young Nation's minds, home of Lewis and Walcott
Intellectuals, luminaries, men of ambition who tasted sea green grape
Past Choc Cemetery, its White Houses and sand pyramids, a long shot.
On the white pages of sand, the rich register of names, signed their time
Our achievements etched on the sea's shimmering script stitched space
Those who read the scriptures and heard lectures on reason and rhyme
Great expectations, tailored ambitions that gave names to every face.

Cain and Abel were brothers when this story began. The brutal beatings
Bending over to touch the straw of the chair while the heavy white hand
Descended on black buttocks, the cane fixating its target, the findings
Of colonial corporal punishment, the same whip on the white massa land.
The taste of cigarettes and rum were not part of the presentation, learnt
That we could experiment, with dice and cards, Clarke's pit seats at Cinema
Our eyes ablaze at the hot kiss on the screen. Hollywood oil lamps burnt
While the coal pots glowing red from its base like a volcanic cyclorama.
The stifling aroma of roasted coffee without milk, prolonged their hours
Examinations opened toll gates of the developing highways, to navigate
Successfully through the cracks and crevices, conflicts marching to wars
Brave gladiators armed in the arena, kill or be killed, try not to hestitate.

I was seventeen, sleeping on the floor with my granny on the double bed
Waking on the morning she would die. I put on white cricket gear in time.
I was wicketkeeping for St. Mary's in the second division, the Police ahead
Of the championship and I kissed her goodbye for the last time, in her prime.
Mindoo Philip umpired the game, put me out leg before wicket, two catches
SMC won on first innings, I was going to tell my grandmother about my game.
As I entered the House, death had snatched her among that day's dispatches
The sad elongated faces of my Father, Uncle, cousins, countenances the same.
Born in Fond St. Jacques, 88 years before she bore my Father in Du Maroni
Cayenne, she wore Wob Dwyet, gold earrings, elegance and in creole style.
Her eyes were my headlamps and I was getting tired of cheese and macaroni
After they placed her in the ground, I cried as she vanished in my sauntering smile.

Within twenty four sleepless hours, I was sleeping in my other grandmother's
Bed in Vieux Fort, took the bus, since I was mesmerized of being in Castries
To the wooden house with its pit toilet across from the Presbytery of Fathers
Frenchmen, who had conquered our minds with mirrors and their ministries.

They who had named the Indians; Coolie A, Coolie B, Coolie C. They preached
Everyday, the strain of their voices echoing in my ears, with the whiff of incense
A clash of Angels with the violence, their voices in discord, cacophony increased
Singing from their Heaven in Latin. Seemed their words made little common sense
To my grandmother, who sold her tall husband's faith, fish, cakes and castor oil
To passersby, while her children took turns at sleeping through Church Service
At most times five to six people, cramped into two beds after a hard day's toil
Snoring in symphonies of African and Creole, swearing at this human sacrifice.

Ma Yette gone and my resurrection after the Cross at Calvary, my empty space
Was fulfilled with the Attorney General's Office, with glasses to see my dream.
I moved to the Treasury to prepare the January Budget in the changing face
Of Politics, then to Post Office duties in Soufriere, the poinsettia's gleam.
Moule a Chique spread its tentacles to the base of the hills hoisted on clouds.
An old Sugar Mill beside a River, where once rice fields grew, comes progress
Its flanks, the changing infrastructure of shanties, empowerment of crowds
From Mang to Bacadere, the stagnant stench of ti kaye, pwevit and stress.
Working blue colour, navy blue suit, bowler hat. "Hi captain, I am ready to go
To London to visit the Queen". Blazing, blessed in plain view of my Father
Who hugged me, his smell of aftershave and cigarettes for I loved him so
At Hewanorra, the Virgin rips the bluescreen, on its way to Heathrow's Tower.

One Love

A Play by Gandolph St. Clair

Dedicated to my Father - Jerome George St. Clair
1913 - 1976

Introduction

GANDOLPH ST. CLAIR 'S One Love was written in 1977 as the Rasta Movement had made its presence felt in the Caribbean spreading since 1966 from Jamaica, where Haile Selaisse had visited that year, the same year that Queen Elizabeth visited the British Colonies including St.Lucia. The play was judged best new play for 1977 winning the Howick Ellcock Memorial Award. It was cited as being existential in its genre. One Love was produced first as a Radio Play in December of that year and subsequently as a stage play in 1978 with Dramaturge Roderick Walcott working with writer/actor/director Gandolph St. Clair. Later that year, there was a TV production directed by Robert Lee. Other actors involved in the production were Earl Bousquet (radio) and George Alphonse (stage and TV) who played the Rasta, Shirley Alexander (radio) and Irma Bushell (stage and TV) who played the girl, Craig Charles who played the second man and Gandolph St. Clair played the first man. Set design and lights were by Roderick Walcott.

Cast of Characters

1st Man
2nd Man
Rasta
Girl
Body

"ONE LOVE"

A ROAD THAT LEADS TO AND FROM A VILLAGE—AN OLD MAN, SLIGHTLY BENT, COMES ON STAGE WEARING DIRTY WHITE TORN-UP SHORT SLEEVED SHIRT AND BLACK LONG PANTS TIED AT THE WAIST WITH A BLUE TIE, BAREFEET, CARRYING A YELLOW HAVERSACK AND WEARING AN OLD STRAW HAT—WITH A CRAZY SHAPED WALKING STICK. HE STOPS ON SEEING A FIGURE SPRAWLED NEAR THE FAR SIDE OF THE ROAD—SUN JUST GOING DOWN—BIRDS CHIRPING.

1st Man: Oh no! Not one of them again—it's hard and tough luck when a man allows non sense like this to happen—just lying there. The sun doesn't worry him—no care in the world—when you're on this open road, you've got to keep moving—why in God's name did he slump there like that?

(MOVES CLOSER TOWARDS BODY AND EXAMINES HIM FROM A DISTANCE AND THEN RETREATS TO THE OPPOSITE SIDE, UNPACKS HIS HAVERSACK AND STARTS EATING HIS BREAD.)

He must be bloody drunk—stone drunk—those drunkards sleep it off any place, any time and as soon as they come around—straight back to it—it's pathetic and disgraceful for human beings, who should have a sense of being—a sense of existence, to waste their precious lives away—alcohol, it's the scourge of this world's society. Hey you—you drunk—you could share my meal with me—forget it—why should I care or worry? I don't even know him but we share the gift of God—I'll wait till he comes through and take him to my shack down the road. Misery, misery that is all this alcohol causes—millions of gallons of misery produced everyday to enslaven the mind and body of millions of people just like that guy. Full utilization of capitalistic power operating just for material development—money—for money, this society will produce anything—do anything—like producing, marketing, advertising alcohol—alcohol, the most devastating drug killer–society is fully aware of the consequences, social, mental and physical, problems that follow after the continued use of alcohol—the broken homes—the senseless crimes committed and yet political aspirants mesmerize their fellowmen with the dream that buildings and voluntary associations will help humanity get rid of the scourge of mankind—alcohol—when it gets you, it makes you it's slave –the American Indians know what made them lose their birthright!

(VOICE SINGING "FOR THE TAINTED WATERS"—2ND MAN ENTERS—STAGGERING WITH HALF BOTTLE OF RUM.)

2nd Man: Eh, how you doing Mister?—what's he doing out there?—I just wouldn't do that!–You see, it's how you hold the liquor—I could drink from now till daybreak and I'd never end up like that.

1st Man: That's funny, very funny. You'd never end up like that but you'd end up worse off—you might be dead.

2nd Man: Dead! *(GOES CLOSE TO PROSTRATE BODY—THEN STOPS).* —You, You want to know why I hit the bottle so hard?—Do you want to know?

1st Man: It just might be interesting—I really won't mind. Care for some of my meal?

2nd Man: Thanks—No thanks—'cos I really don't think I could eat off another person's sweat—that would make me a parasite—besides I don't even know you, but I'll let you in on my secret—I drink because I'm lonely. The biggest hurt in the world, loneliness—no wife—she's gone after sixteen years of marriage—what a life it was—brought three kids up—they gone as well. I'd give up the bottle if they'd come back—but what the hell—no man ought to beg—a man should stand the suffering—take the pain—the hurt—but, just can't do without the bottle—I just can't—shit, I feel so helpless, where's my courage? Where's my strength? It's only when I see, those in a worse position than myself—like that guy—that I see, how bad my position is—a few minutes ago I was happy—without a God-damned care in this world—now seeing him like that, has brought everything back to mind.

(MOVES OVER TO 1ST MAN AND SITS BESIDES HIM).

I won't mind some of your bread, if you still feel like sharing.

1st Man: Oh no—I don't mind, the offer is still open, help yourself.

2nd Man: Thanks. Life is one whole orbit of confusion—birth, born out of wedlock—a scarred reputation—bastard the society calls you—but now who cares—it don't matter if you're the son of Mr. & Mrs.—or of that lady and that mister—it's who you are that matters—that's the way it should be—once born you enter this world with the same gift as everybody else—the gift of God—life and death—life, when we get into orbit and death when we get out—between life and death there's marriage, children, you have to put up with those in whose orbit, you may at some point, cross, personal relationships—some value money for everything -forget charity—the old are abused and mistreated—there's war, greed, hatred, there's injustice, inequality—before death comes you find discrimination—the color of the skin, what does it matter?—Which one of us can see the Spirit? Yet black fight white—white fight black—those days everybody's busy at the conference table stalling for time. In the twinkling of an eye—one minute, we could be here and the next, oblivion—nuclear weapons ain't no joke—all the riches and money for which we kill—steal—cheat, all the false pleasures for which we commit a million and one sins against God and man—all the temporary comforts, which we selfishly protect for own personage to the extreme of waste–all these things are inconsequential.....nothing....I find myself in a world of despair—having only this (referring to booze) is my hope.

1st Man: How can you put all hope and trust in liquor? What about the Godliness you spoke of not too long ago, I only wish that our friend had heard you—might have been able to make him give up what you're now calling your hope—preachers do not practice what they preach—the simplest commandment—love one another—is easy on the lips, but hardest in practice, because like you say, we value the comforts, the pleasure, the riches so much so—that any obstacle in the way must be destroyed, and battles to be fought, won at any price—pride and pomp in our victories make us unforgiving to our vanquished—continual aggression and oppression until we wipe the enemy out of the earth, but what's the war for? There's nothing to be gained, only suffering—to so many, this life is the only way it seems, the beginning and the end—once I've come close to the end—the days we spent on the sea—just sky and water—twenty one days of mental torture, hunger, like a director showed the way—we all seemed mad—each lost in his own thoughts—Who'd be to blame? Would anybody ever find us?—Three dead bodies in a boat on the high seas—Pasco couldn't come to grips with it at first, but he gradually took it in when he died. Was telling stories, he laughed at the cricket match, he remembered from his youth—when he square-cut to the man at point, who tried to stop a bullet from the bat and ended up with a visible brown patch on the rear of his white flannels—the crowd erupted as the player had to run off to change his trousers—I can see Pasco's face as he went through his last smiles on earth. He had found the strength and courage to face death. Faith is all-important a factor—when all seems lost, it's only if we have faith in God that we overcome problems—human beings lack faith—you lack faith so you turn to alcohol—I have been found wanting in my strength too, but who doesn't at sometime or other, feel lost in this plague of inhumanity and suffering which has conquered the world—religion, religion—fanatic uncontrollable organizations, eating out the hearts of men and cushioning the hopes of weaklings. This world has come to a long way to its sad, sorry state—men's hearts have become temples of hate and jealousy—their actions, cornerstones of greed and selfishness and believe me—Mister, I walk the open road to keep away from mankind—but it's futile—as long as you're living, you'll meet all types, even on the open road—a drunk—

2nd Man: Two—one half drunk and one stone cold drunk—how long has he been there?

1st Man: I've been here for sometime and I found him there, so I guess he'll soon come through.

2nd Man: Maybe we should wake him.

1st Man: I don't think, we should we disturb him and bring him back to his world of misery just now—if you're not in a hurry, we two could await his awakening—by the way, where you off to? I live not far from here in a shack I built for myself—I call it my tomb.

2nd Man: I've got to get to the next village before noon tomorrow to check on a job—but I'm broke—penniless—so I'm using my legs 'cos I can't afford bus fare—this bottle of booze is on account of my good name—credit—until I come into the money bag again—it's been three years that way, running from everyone I owe—and I can't get a job—just can't get a job.

1st man: How about your friends?

2nd Man: Friends, eh! 'Twas a long time ago—but at the end of it, we know that friends are there when the going's good; when it's rough they're gone—when you are unemployed, its like you've got a deadly virus and society automatically shuns you—it's hurtful when I remember all those that I've helped when I could and now there's nobody to help me –not even rum friends. But again, who can help me if I don't help myself—now even my strength is gone, gone—how can you cope with life after sixteen years of what you thought was love, happiness, your best friend—the man to whom you open your door to everyday—the man who knows your ins and outs, every—thing about you—a man you'd trust and you'd defend for eternity—when that man comes up against you—what my eyes saw was horror and what I did they called it terror—I tried to kill the bastard—I'd always lusted after my wife and when I found out what was going on, it was a crazy hate—I spent six months of sheer hell trying to keep my sense in the crazy world they'd fitted me in, when it was I who'd been wronged—what kept me sane was the fact that I was convinced that the whole damn society was mad—I spent two years in jail serving my sentence for bodily harm—two years hard labor—two years of routine frustration—I got pay rolled early to come back to this (INDICATING BOTTLE)—the family has gone clean out of my life—I was a criminal at the end of years of decent, honest living—so now what do I need to worry about friends for?—It's been four years of booze and paid women, on and off—tell me, friend, do you see any justice in this life?

1st Man: All justice, my friend, has long since lost its meaning, because the power of trust is and can be replaced by money and favor—I was on the right side of the law or so I thought—until it dawned on me that everybody was busy breaking the laws of God—no penalty as yet—but when you break man's laws you'll be penalized; men therefore live by their laws, not God's; but man is subject to God—I gave up their uniforms and I headed for the sea to try to find my inner self—I have found that solitude is communion, amid the horror of war, concrete jungles fettered with hypocrites who subject their power on other's, amid the mania of material struggle, where dog eat dog, and hens eat cockroach. Solitude is communion with God—that's why I shack alone, away from everything and everybody.

2nd Man: But that's phony—how can you live like that—no woman—no children?

1st Man: Oh, that side—the backside—women, lots of them and in the end—I won—no woman. When I came back from the sea—I hustled like any other guy for the material things—I got them car, house and beautiful women—I remember Sheila, a woman who was as simple as love itself—giving but not in the hope of receiving—it was good that while—but then she turned wrong—I gave what I could but she wanted more and so we lost our degree of balance—love should always be allowed to find it's own level—I leave one son—my image—you know what he is? A Rasta—Rasta—he have brains to stand talk with the Devil self—but he and I won't share views or news—but I love him—I love him and he knows that's all I live for now—for the reconciliation—when—when—it was I who fathered him, when he challenged the social and moral values of society—gave up Secondary School, turned Ras—I was shattered, I'd been a Babylon, my life-long regret—my inner being today is the Rasta heart itself.

2nd Man: My only son is a Rasta too, that generation is being stifled—no jobs after years of schooling, the type of education—foreign—questionable—baffling—the concept of honesty and charity was absent from the society—still is—mediocrity, complacency was to have been the order of the day—now that they're shaking the foundations of society—the daughters and sons of the top class have the same guns pointing at their heads—he alone of my family cares for me and I don't see him that often—look man, one of dem Ras coming with his daughter—By the way, what's your name?

1st Man: What's in a name?

(RASTA IN JEANS AND BOB MARLEY T-SHIRT AND PREGNANT GIRL WEARING MATERNITY DRESS AND TAM ENTER—SILENCE—STARES AMONG PLAYERS—THEN THE EYES OF EVERYBODY FOCUS ON THE BODY—A CRY OF HORROR DISTURBS EVERYTHING—THE GIRL RUNS AND TURNS THE BODY OVER AND FALLS PROSTATE ON THE BODY—FIRST MAN GRABS AT RASTA AND SHAKES HIM—TRYING TO FIND OUT THE CONNECTION BETWEEN THE BODY AND THE GIRL.)

1st Man: *(TO RASTA)* What's the girl to him?

Rasta: What is you to me?

1st Man: What is your name?

2nd Man: What's in a name? *(MOVES OVER TO GIRL.)*

Rasta: What's in a name? You is my father and you in your evil vibration can't check I—you can't recognize I—is later for you. *(RASTA MOVES OVER TO GIRL.)*

1st Man: My son, my son—Boy, I want to talk to you—man, man, I want to tell you that I'm sorry—ask for your forgiveness—it was only as I tried to understand your spirit that I understood my own as I had to reach mine before I could reach yours.

Rasta: Rest a while Sar—me daughter in a grief—me don't know why, Sar—so rest na—until later *(PAUSE)* He's dead.

2nd Man: What happen dere?

1st Man: Dead? One after the other—dead—shit—but no, no—I thought he was asleep—death comes when all the songs are being sung and poems being read—why must it unshackle the hearts of men and make the living pitiable creatures? I understand your grief, your loss, lady—the sorrow in your heart is in mine and in my friend's—we were waiting to take him along with us along the road when he came through, but death has played a joke on us helpless creatures—death alone can conquer time which life has given to us—those tears that you shed are the rains of death—like the smiles that greet birth are the rays of the sunshine of life—there is joy in death—Death is the beginning of another life, so take heart—Dust thou art, to dust thou shall return—the same breath which gives life must depart from the body—we come to this world with nothing and leave all, everything behind—we all have accepted the gift of God, that is why we are born—life and death—but during life, we forget that this life on earth, will and must end—we fail to understand this condition of creation.

Rasta: Daughter, is so the man had to die—on the road because that was his home, corn a him ital—free up, tears nuh bring him back—love up—live up *(PULLS HER OFF THE BODY—DAUGHTER SOBS UNCONTROLLABLY IN THE RASTA'S ARMS.)*

1st Man: Son, I'm sorry.

Rasta: Sorry? What for, Sar—you still a weak heart—what happen here was due to happen so don't dig pon it—take it easy, daughter, easy.

2nd Man: What relation was the man to your daughter, Rasta man?

Rasta: How you expect I and I to know—she can't talk—daughter, free up—free up—get yourself together!

Daughter: My father's dead—dead—Oh Papa!

1st Man: What a coincidence—I have found my son after all these years—his daughter has lost her father. After searching for all these years, Son, we have a second chance to communicate our love—it is a fate that brings us here today—I know that I've wronged you but it's in our hearts that we can forgive—I didn't understand your rebellion, rejection of all the things I stood for—but you are right—the way of life is the way of the spirit and not material—son, I must talk to you after this thing is sorted out.

Rasta: I go listen to you, Sar—the light of Jah Rastafari will shine pon you—if you true—but if you're a jokey—the light will destroy you, like in the times before in a Babylon—the time you throw me out of your place and insult my mother and me—is only if your word true, Jah will make I forget them evilous oppression and forgive you.

2nd Man: Do we help get the body moved or let you talk your lives away?—let's organize to get him back to the village.

Rasta: Daughter, leh we organize to move—where him used to live?

Daughter: De mister no have home Sar, no relative except me one—him left me since small—gone immigration to England, spend sixteen years never check I—then he commit apostasy—marry Honky—come bring her back, let sweet boy in de place, flirt on him and thing—always a white man come down to check she—is always she cousin and she always in a hotel and he 'pon de road—all him little money going, the Honky controlling it—make he fart but she never like me—I straighten her out every time—it was through that, me that break up their relationship—I bring a partner home and she dig up 'pon he—and like what she want she gets—when my father get to know it—he raving mad. Want to chop me pardner—ah tell me old man is not so—open your eyes, I hail him and I open dem for him and he see so much, he run her off to England but not before he was broke—I tell he every instance of the games the honky lady play 'pon he and I watch him face full up with rage and regret—is about a year now since the lady gone back to England—bank seize property and he turn to liquor real hard. Malgadi start to take mister, he start make de open sky his road—he stop eat, he forget he need clothes, he forget to bathe unless the open sky favors him, crazy, with nothing except, what he have on him—that red shirt that I hustle from a pardner I gave it to him three months ago when I last saw him—now he's dead—stone cold gone—that's crazy—I tried to talk him into giving up the booze, so he promised me, he go to the country by some fellow to cool things off—that's how it ends—sixty—two—unknown—un-cherished—unwanted—what a place to die—the open road.

1st Man: Don't worry everything will be taken care of—You have seen the main reason why I live the way I do—I shack alone—given up the material things of the world because my reason guided me to seek the truth in this existence—Love, one love is the truth—I need your love—look son—how about giving it a try—you and your daughter could rest by me, for a few weeks until we sort things out?

Rasta: Daughter—Jah Rastafari works wonder, thanks and praises—we get a place to cool out for a while—the baby will not be born on the road—Yes, Sar, I go check you after we sort de mister body.

2nd Man: But how will you go about getting the body out from here?

Daughter: Ras tell you that, you and his father go carry it back to the village-is endless scene with dem people—back dere—dey go want to know how him dead—what him die of—questions that have no answers.

Rasta: Let dem ask questions—Daughter, don' keep dem things in studiation—free up—I have a white sheet in my bag, so if you organize the body we could start.

(FIRST MAN TAKES SHEET FROM RASTA AND PASSES IT TO SECOND MAN).

2nd Man: Rasta, so how you won't touch the dead?

Rasta: Mister, you like to talk too much—it's I and I personal conviction—so free up—so what you doing?

(AS THE TWO MEN TRY TO ORGANISE IN A POSITION FOR WRAPPING UP THE BODY.)

2nd Man: But Rasta, you think, that two of us—your father and I can manage this thing?—What belief can you possibly have for not wanting to help move the body—Rasta, where's your reason? I understand perhaps the causes for your running off on society—but your dreadness cannot be exercised against a corpse—the soul have long since left the body—why don't you stop messing around and give us a hand?—It's getting late—when sun set my services can no longer be available.

Rasta: So you apply your principle after sundown—I and I apply principle all the while—I and I not carrying no dead body—rest up.

2nd Man: Beg you come and give me hand with the body?

Rasta: Me Sar—no way—this is just a carcass nothing—the spirit live on leaving the body—Rastaman no meddle, mister.

1st Man: So what are we gonna do?

Rasta: Make I tell you—two of you can carry the mister body.

2nd Man: But you're stronger than the two of us!

Rasta: If I stronger than the two of you—then is Jah love that make I and I so—is my meditation that make I survive—when my belly turn and twist—is I and I one know it—strength is wisdom. Rasta strength that make I survive Babylon—when they take me in for burnin' natural marijuana—cut off my locks—that was strength eh? They think so but Jah Rastafari children must be free-from worry and want, from evil and corruption—free from poverty and starvation. Hunger does not breed human beings of equal right—Zion is the land when Rasta belong—Mister, where that man try to impress upon you that he is my father—Father, what did you do for me? *(SILENCE)* You see—but yet still you believe that there is hope for us to reconcile our differences. Well my list of differences are grievances, because I was wronged by you—how can you put that right? Parents always believe that they know what's good for their children and forget that the child or youth have a life of their own to live—me daughter father gone bust because his reason was wrong—he was lucky that he know how his money gone before he dead—action without reason is treason—so you must pay—you never even stop to think that I would grow up big?—Like your friend say have strength.

1st Man: I don't even know how to start to say it, but I feel remorse in my heart, on two counts this day—one this mister, it was I who came across him first—I assumed that he was drunk—so preachers don't practice what they preach—I who often think of the true concept of charity how its missing in our society, I failed a fellow human being—but on your count, Son I must not fail you—son I will not fail you—Where her mother?

1st Man *(TO 2ND MAN)*: You must not worry about him—let's try our best and maybe we will make it –he's young and strong headed—but he's a man—he was only sixteen, when he nearly send me off my head but that was three years ago when I suppose my own head needed examining. Three long years, today's the first day since we've seen each other in that much time—Son you look different?

Rasta: Yes, Sar, I feel different and you different too—that what time is supposed to do us—sight?

2nd Man: The body! The damn dead body! Why can't you help? The two of us won't ever be able to get to the Village before sunset. Rasta, I have son that Rasta too—but he not like you.

Rasta: All man different.

2nd Man: But all Rasta have one philosophy—one love—but that ain't love, when you tell me that this dead man's daughter carries your unborn child—without this man, you'd never have this chance to be a father—without this dead man's gift of God to him—how could God share his gift with you?—Rasta, you've said action without reason is treason—you're committing treason by not helping us.

1st Man: Son, be realistic—what harm can it do you—if you help! You have mingled in his blood—you—me—we are all one–one love–one cause–one joy—one Creator—one Conqueror—why? Why? Look at her–tears–as you shred sinews of love–it is eating up her heart—why don't you help her?—help us!—the living bury the dead—not the dead, bury the dead.

2nd Man: What could be your conviction?

1st Man: You know full, well that it's about time we get going—we'll have to call a Doctor from the village to find out how he died—autopsy—post mortem—love! Must I lose faith after what I've learnt through your actions, son?

Rasta: *(PAUSES)* Let's go *(GOES TO DAUGHTER.)*

2nd Man: At long last.

1st Man: Let's make it fast.

Rasta: One love.

(EXIT THE THREE MEN CARRYING BODY IN CLOTH- LED BY DEAD MAN'S DAUGHTER.)

Guess who came to visit the Doctor?

A Play by Gandolph St. Clair

Dedicated to the St. Lucia Nurses Association

Introduction

Written for the St. Lucia Nurses Association in 1978. The play was staged in New Jersey, in the same year by the Gulf Theatre Workshop directed by Irvin Grey, with a St.Lucian cast and later that year, the play was produced by Trinidad & Tobago's The Strolling Players, directed by Freddie Kisson.

Characters-in order of appearance

Angie-Receptionist
Mrs. Bertram-1st Visitor
Christine-2nd Visitor
Daniel-3rd Visitor
Esther-4th Visitor
Dr. John Finchley

The Scene:

A Doctor's front office with desk for the receptionist, small filing cabinet near desk, receipt book, appointment book and telephone. Six chairs and a table with reading material, pictures and an almanac on wall.

Enter Angie wearing her expensive aquamarine mini outfit and her hair style, sporting a bun, wearing gold bracelets, chain with cross, rings, earrings, make up, high heels.

Angie: What! Twenty five past eight, I bet he's in there already *(puts down hand bag and picks up phone)* Good morning Doctor, You're in early. Oh I see. I see thanks for the gift. How about tonight? No problem. No problem, Anytime you want. At what time will you be ready for your patients? Ok, whenever. *(places receiver down)* Daytime friends, Night time lovers, What a secret no one will ever discover.

Mrs Bertram: *(Walks in from side to side in an oversized large red knee length dress.)*
This thing does move! Morning! This baby does move child! I had Mr.Bertram drive us here this morning. He give me this baby; put me in this way, and now he trying hard to run away from responsibilities.

Angie: But Mrs. Bertram, I thought it would be a whole lot different since you married!

Mrs.Bertram: This thing does move, and is when you married, it different. You does depend on the man, you know. He is the one to depend on. ... so you tie up you belly early. First thing, when Bertram know he had put me so, he start go out more regular, is more phone call, late night and he stop sleep by me like a had a malady, that is what hard. When that is hard to get, a little comfort, things is bad, my fourth pregnancy but it seems like my first.

Angie: Think you should know by now what to expect of Mr.Bertram. *(Looks at cards.)* My name is Angie...I new here... for today... Angie... see a ghost?

Mrs.Bertram: Expect of Mr.Bertram, since when you hear man does expect? It's me that expecting and all the man do every time is come round, knock on my belly and he showing his teeth all over, "it kicking already?" Angie, you say; you know Bertram so bold face, one day, when I was expecting my second, he put his head by my belly and Bertram say, the child kick so hard, he thought was me give him a punch. That man does lie!

Angie: *(laughs)* Mrs.Bertram, ah there's your card! I see the Doctor has seen you so many times before and is your family doctor, expensive taste and the best. They say he is the best. Here's your card.

Mrs.Bertram: Best? Der aint have nuttin so Angie, how you mean? Maybe Doctor Finchley making the most money but dat doan make him the best Doctor. Is God that give him to do, all dat he doing. Is God is the best Doctor. If the patient ain't have faith, nothing doing.

Angie: I always full of faith in God but Dr.Finchely not counting in that. All those men just coming to fool people, I prefer the older men, they more expensive and they making more sense. They can take care of you better.

Mrs.Bertram: That embryo can kick, Ok na I know you there! When can I see the doctor?

Angie: Soon!

Mrs.Bertram: I hope Bertram remember to come and pick me up, that man so forgetful that it is pitiful. You new here you say for one day? How old are you, Angie?

Angie: *(laughs)* This morning the baby really making you talk. I'm nineteen, single and disengaged. Six GCE! No Maths! It is my first day here!

Mrs.Bertram: Nineteen, sweet age, you look way mature I must say. There's a young girl coming. Angie don't you people ever change those Time magazines? I forget you new here but I go read something all the same.

Enter Christine (appears to have been crying. Christine wears plaid skirt, white shirt and sneakers. Hair in plaits. Carries sling purse.)

Christine: *(Goes to receptionist)* Good morning. Would like to see the Doctor please! First time!

Angie: OK *(pulls out index card - hand to Christine)*. Just fill it out please and have a seat. You go in after Mrs.Bertram. Pay the Doctor!

Christine: Thanks! *(Blows her nose, then seats herself next to Mrs.Bertram, as she picks up a copy of a Time.)*

(Angie appears to be looking at some files, Mrs.Bertram is reading then she slams the magazine down.)

Mrs.Bertram: You must really tell Finchley to change those old magazines. A big doctor like that can afford to buy up to date classy magazines and papers. How people go get educated, when you have these same old papers there all the time? If he ain't giving de latest, at least change them!. Ah go tell him that myself. Shame on Dr. Finchley!

Angie: I hear they say pregnant women like to talk a lot, that seems true.

Mrs.Bertram: *(laughs, stares at Christine as she hands index card to Angie after filling it out.)* Eh, eh, that's Christine? Mrs. Tenham daughter!

Angie: You're right Mrs.Bertram, Christine Tenham's the name. You know everybody?

Mrs.Bertram: Angie, I been around so I know people but ah does mind my business. Mrs. Tenham and I goan school together at the Ave Maria Girls Primary, so ah know she features and ah doan forget it. I know when she born, her mother make her at sixteen. Her mother same age with me. How are you, Christine? What happen to you?

Christine: I suppose to answer you?

Mrs.Bertram: How you mean?

Christine: You done publicize my entry into the world and you think you really care, how I feeling now? You never care before, first time I meet you in my life, in a Doctor's office. You want to know my business? Is people like you all, dat doan mind your business, dat causing all dis confusion. If I tell you, my business, then you go give your own version to somebody else.

Mrs.Bertram: Eh, eh, look at the child un. I does mind my business. Eh, eh, but you know how it is these days. Anytime you see a young girl go and visit Doctor is Abortion.

Angie: Not inside here Mrs.Bertram. You must watch what you saying, that's an illegal thing you talking about there.

Christine: Same thing again, you have your big belly, I ain diggin nutthin on you. I ain askin you, if de man take it, but you believe I come here for Abortion. You all ain know what you all want. They don't want Family Planning. They don't want Abortion. They don't want you to get educated about Sex. They don't want you to have boyfriend. My mother does send my sister everywhere I going and does ask her all types of stupid question, about who I talk to. Dem old people causing all de confusion.

Angie: Is time that put de confusion!

Mrs.Bertram: Is people that put de confusion. De older people use to have to make sure, it was love before they go to bed because they had to know what kind of men they dealing with, but now the young people are well protected, so everything is just fun. Look at how marriage does break up.

Angie: I done say I ain getting married to no man yet. I young and I enjoying it. Them men only want your body to possess it, that's theirs and they want to move around. They know how to use and abuse woman, and if you even talk to a man is trouble. I Angie say, no man pushing me in no dark hole. I free up once the scene is tight, I hold you right and to hell with love. I love myself.

Mrs.Bertram: Love does exist ? Young girls, you think they have that again? Is money, metal and material, the three M's of modernity depending on how much you have you running woman. Lawyers, Doctors, Police, Insurance men, Salesman, Drug man, dem at the top, them is playboys dat have car and nice clothes and their deep pockets. Dem necks choking dem with gold and diamond, then all man not same, even if dey have six woman to one man population ratio. Some woman does run six men.

Angie: Women leaving the men behind, like in hare and tortoise race...they burning fast..that is not when we used to carry Coal, Sugar Cane and Banana...

Christine: Occupational habits ! What you think does make them do it? Society. Society that gone mad... From the time you twelve de men calling you, for you to get a job is trouble, if you not bending down, you staying on de ground.

Angie: I didn't have to bend!

Mrs.Bertram: Who knows?

Angie: Mrs. Bertram is time you go and see de Doctor!

Mrs.Bertram: *(gets up to move)* There's a handsome young man! *(Daniel comes on wearing short blue short sleeved shirt, yellow tie, black pants, clean shaven with haircut, shining black shoes. Watch, bangle on right wrist.)*

Angie: Mrs.Bertram!

Mrs.Bertram: Okay this thing does kick! *(Enters Doctor's office.)*

Daniel: Is somebody tell her eat pigeon peas with garlic? I want see de Doctor, dear.

Angie: First time visiting? How dear do you think I am?

Daniel: First time! Dearly! Dare me?

Angie: Fill out that card and have a seat. Christine, you musn't worry about people like this. Mrs. Bertram! They just want to know everybody business and they ain have no time for their own business. Her husband have two outside women. She ain include Civil Servants in the list of men that controlling women. Everynight he in strip Club!

Christine: Fighting class Civil Servants, inside and outside - strikes and pay hikes!

Daniel: Man that think they controlling women, no man can control woman. My philosophy as a man is take them as they come. When a man put a woman in his head he might as well be dead. Give her everything but yet still they does turn bad. Sometimes I does wonder, if woman is the devil on earth!

Christine: Is you man that is the devil! Is man does start war, start victimize and oppress people. Start and encourage weak minds to do evil deeds, is man dat does tell lie about everything. Man dat is de devil..

Daniel: Maybe de man dat you have is a devil! Evil?

Christine: Ah just finish tell dat lady, I ain discussing my business with nobody. You is a man! Ah fraid you tongue more than a woman tongue.

Angie: Dat chick really dread. How you could dread up de man so. You all was just reasoning!

Daniel: She just checking she own self and that is necessary for everybody to do, but she can't take it out on me. I ain ask you, your business you know sista. Ah come here to get some time off a work because dem people trying to overwork me. Abuse me! My two other pardners on sick leave. All we dere go be on sick leave. Sista, so much things does happen to man, that make we sweat and we does take kicks, and cannot move but some of them like it so... so them get it. People doesn't take time out for themselves, to check their movements as to why things does happen. Why some have to call a red sunset, by another colour? If you can see the sunset, its many colours, that is what you want to see. You say what you see. It is no trouble. Be cool sister; maybe you've been hurt by one man. So all man ain good?

Angie: All man ain de same. All dey same a woman has got to show her independence. Don't give all of you to any man because they don't know how to appreciate that. When you give too much they does abuse it!

Christine: I ain care how you want to see it, whether all man same or all man not same. Nobody ain confusing me. Them people because of what they do with their lives already, done mess it up already, they afraid to see you do different and settle with your life. Things getting worse. You cannot get a job after you finish School, then you have to stay home and find yourself open to exploitation and sexploitation. Do that and it nice. But when you say you not staying locked in by the fear, which dominated our parents and you break tradition, which controlled our parents' minds, you no good. But, that is survival!

Daniel: Like dat man give you real horrors. He make you look at reality, whereas some people just depend on something to happen.

Christine: Which man that you talking about? Some live only in fantasies and dreams, refuse to accept change and progress. They see only the visible progress in things that dem can see and such things material, but spiritual and collective growth dat ain counting no way. All that people have time for is setting brother against brother by gossiping. If you ain clapping with them they chanting you down. Man jealous of man, dog eat dog. So both me and you stick in this life. Survival is no different! It's the game!

(Out comes Mrs. Bertram from Doctor's office. Daniel gives card to Angie.)

Mrs.Bertram: So you all still discussing? *(stop at desk.)*

Christine: Discussing not fussing and cussing *(gets up to go to Doctor's office)* Why you doan just go about your business?

Angie: Not yet Christine!

Mrs. Bertram: Dat thing still kicking. See that man Bertram aint come to meet me.

Angie: If it was somebody else he'd be waiting.

Daniel: Ever try to mind read?

Mrs. Bertram: I left school in fourth standard!

Daniel: Infant or Primary?

Mrs. Bertram: Secondary!

Angie: You have form.

Christine: Mama - Just cheese, please!

Daniel: Must have been quite an Education?

Mrs. Bertram: Woman doan really need Education just to be a housewife and have children. Think that call for GCE? Alphabets and Roman numerals!

Christine: The other way around! Roman numerals and Alphabets!

Angie: How you people could think so? You hear of woman liberation. Equal rights for woman, no wonder you always so!

MrS.Bertram: How you mean?

Angie: You always pregnant! So you think that is what all woman dere for?

Daniel: A lot of man see it so. The way dey see it but it's women of themselves, who have brought the yoke to bear upon themselves. Give women their place let them be heard in business, in professions, in the Church.

Mrs. Bertram: In da Church?

Angie: Why not?

Christine: World War One, then World War Two.

Daniel: In politics!

Angie: It's fear that keeping them back!

Daniel: Not fear but women seem to do less thinking of themselves than men, so you find, they are less aware and hence their continual dependence on the whims and fancies of man!

Angie: Make you feel good? Eh!

Daniel: Na! it make me feel sad!

Mrs. Bertram: I don't even have a blasted twenty five dollar let me hire a taxi! The doctor take all my money. You must be getting a fat salary. Angie de Doctor making $25 a minute!

Angie: You bound to be sick if you aint talk about some body business!

Christine: Lively up yourself, Ma Bertram!

Daniel: Karn help it!

Mrs. Bertram: How you know so? I karn help it, I have to know, to be on the go. When they discussing mine, think I don't want discuss them too! *(horn blows)*

Angie: That must be your Bertram! - Your turn Christine! *(Christine goes in.)*

Mrs. Bertram: You think she pregnant?

Angie: You expect me to know?

Daniel: She not de doctor!

Mrs.Bertram: I wish, I was de doctor just to know that for sure!

Angie: Trying asking her when she comes out *(Horn blows.)*

Mrs. Bertram: Well I go have to go and I ain know whether she pregnant. She careful in she talk, I goin. Next time I come, make sure you all change dem old Time magazine, ah gone *(bumps into Esther as she makes her exit)*. Mind your business.

(Esther enters wearing a pink print pants suit, with head scarf, high pink heels, stockings. She goes straight into a waiting chair without addressing anybody, setting her four parcels down at her feet.)

Esther: Oh God I am tired!

Daniel: Looks like you been running away. Found you couldn't do it.

Angie: Can I help you?

Esther: As a prospective patient for your Doctor?

Angie: Yes! Did you come to visit the doctor?

Esther: I'm awfully tired, so I thought the Doctor's office would be a nice place to catch my breath!

Angie: But you can't stay - not to cool your breath!

Esther: Who said I can't stay? Who knows, I might just be staying till visiting hours are over. I'm awfully tired my car is down.

Angie: What's that gotta do with me? I've got a job to do to inquire about everybody who visits. Make sure they get the service they seek. Did you come to visit the doctor?

Esther: I've told you. I'm feeling tired!

Daniel: De lady has a right to stay here, if she wants to.

Angie: What you know about rights?

Daniel: I know, that she ain doing nothing wrong by sitting down where she is. That's what I know about rights, I know a little about citizens' rights because I'm a policeman.

Angie: I know so (goes back to her desk) that's how you have rights, want to enjoy the tax payers' money, coming and look for sick leave.

Daniel: That is my business but that is how that roo roo does work, you tell somebody about your condition and then later they condition you about your condition. That's life!

Esther: *(To Daniel)* Care for a cigarette?

(Christine comes out of Doctor's Office, sobbing and walks straight out.)

Angie: You cannot smoke here!

Daniel: No thanks. I don't smoke, that girl love problems.

Angie: Everybody have problems, you better go in, Mr. Policeman, let me deal with this shady lady!

Daniel: Go easy on her. *(Daniel enters Doctor's office.)*

Esther: Doctors are very special people they see everybody in private, for what goes on behind closed doors nobody knows.

Angie: Have something against Doctors?

Esther: They're necessary!

Angie: You're married?

Esther: I heard that lady say something about minding your business, do that for a change.

Angie: Are you going to see the Doctor?

Esther: Eventually! Personally!

Angie: Well fill out that form!

Esther: I don't think I need to do that!

Angie: Please yourself but remember you haven't got much time in fact that gentleman was to have been our last patient!

Esther: Thanks for the information. I am tired!

(Angie is busy clearing her desk and Esther doses off. Daniel comes out of Doctor's office)

Daniel: Seven days that's it, young lady you mustn't mind people business so!

Angie: You too must be careful not to talk your private business in public places, among unfamiliar faces. See you.

Daniel: I can take that advice from you? Can I have your private number? I need a night nurse. I am on sick leave. Call you to cure me? See you later, bye *(exit)*.

Angie: You must fill in the form! This is your last chance to see the Doctor!

Esther: Oh you are very annoying. I'm trying to relax and you keep on harassing me about the Doctor. I'll see him when I want and this is not my last chance!

Angie: We're closing soon!

Esther: Go ahead then when you are ready. I'll be leaving then just as well *(phone rings)*.

Angie: Hello! That's all for the day!

Esther: Visiting hours very short today!

Angie: It's just some lady who's just catching her breath, she says she is tired. Name? I don't know her. She's leaving soon.

Esther: How soon?

Angie: No lunch today? Later? Tonight? It's always like that. I will not starve! Have it your way! *(Puts receiver down)* Pig!

Esther: He does that to me sometimes!

Angie: What!

Esther: Never mind. (Doctor finally comes out) There you are John Finchely. I thought you'd never come out of office. Let's go! The car broke down and so I thought, I just wait till you're ready to go home! Aren't you going to tell your charming receptionist good bye? Get the parcels John!

Exit John and Esther.

- CURTAIN -

The Patent Man

A Short Story by Gandolph St. Clair

Dedicated to Malcolm "Locks" Magaron

Introduction

THE PATENT MAN was first performed in 1985 with Irvin Norville as Narrator, Eric Branford as Beeple and Patsy Cadet as the Blackbird at Sandals Halcyon. Music composed by Gandolph St. Clair, performed by Connie Marshall, Kennedy Evelyn.

THE PATENT MAN

Beeple was 150 years old. Black, negroid. His hair had aged, withering whitish grey; his skin tissue wrinkled like parchment. He was blind and had revoked his power of speech.

This strange man lay immobile in a sack cloth hammock, forty feet high, suspended from a bamboo pole, between the higher adjacent branches of two giant almond trees on a desolate beach at Air. The rushing waves lashed the sandy shore and the winds whirred amid the trees. The sun scaled the walls of cloud to peer at Beeple. The Sun would have to wait. Its eye could not find Beeple beneath the shade of almond branches.

On the horizon soared a speck, black, in flight against the haze of a boundless expanse of firm blue sky. A blackbird soon nestled at the edge of the hammock and saw the piece of stale bread in the near skeletal hand of Beeple. The blackbird was hungry so it began pecking the bread. The black, gold and white in the blackbird's head now had a point of focus in the cold ashen eyes of the man. The white long shirt and underwear was all that Beeple wore. Beeple had been waylaid into this rigidity having angered the authorities as he was half way through his life. He had created this demise, by not contributing to the process of creation. As a member of the Sea tribe, one had to ensure continuance of race through coitus. On the day of enumeration, he had no family to register. Half of his life had been spent in this art of exile and banishment; this punishment. Even if Beeple had once learnt to plead for mercy and forgiveness, this act of grace to end his tribulation had never come and so negated his sense of feeling, now having been long forgotten and abandoned by his tribe. Beeple thought that the bird pecking his hand was a sign for him to speak.

Beeple spoke in a dead language. "From whence I came I know not and it is not a shame, that I should know not of my birth, save my sire. Where I must go, I know not and where I am, I now know as Air. My hunger eternal, my thirst unsatiable. I have long since forgotten the color of the sun and the hue of night. My memory savors no deity save the cold wet rain and burning sun. My energy a timeless spasm springing from the hearth of the heart."

"You living creature that listens to the melody of my voice, if you must be my deliverer, take me to the Palace of Time, that I may make my final speech. I seek deliverance. Light, peace and justice, there. This three pronged God, whom I must appraise, for the pleasure and the pain of the journey . Are you my deliverer? Speak!"

The Blackbird spread its wings and flew to Beeple's other palm. From the passage beneath its tail flowed momentously a café au lait substance.

Beeple continued in a somnolent voice. "In your silence I heard nothing but the sound of my aged heart pumping, blood. My life's source. My hand feels warm with your substance. Shall we go?"

The blackbird did not reply. It flew upward to the highest almond leaves. Then the old man folded his arms, the clouds grew grey and dark. The Sun hid its face. The rain pelted the leaves.

The blackbird sang. "I am the carrier of your soul
I am the bearer of your whole.
Skin, bone, flesh and spirit, I carry the scroll, the story with it!"

Beeple replied;
"This story is old. Don't ask me to tell the story. I wait. I planted corn, made bread; cut wood, made coal; dug the earth, planted flowers; harnessed bees to make honey! I cast at the sea's edge, my net and I made my bed out of straw. I never dallied on the Sun, Moon and Star to flex muscle and as my eyes never served their purpose –no tears at birth, no laughter at death. I wait. Take me." The rain ceased.

Beeple was drenched. The blackbird thirsty. It flew on Beeple's forehead and began drinking the water out of the sockets of his eyes. Beeple twitched anxiously. "I never saw the mountains, nor the valleys or the rivers that find their way to the sea. The rainbow housed my possession of dreams, without any science, without an Industry."

The Blackbird drained water from Beeple's eyelids, flew to an almond branch and sang:
"Salty tears lace a ready smile
hearty fears grace a sturdy chile.
No more red wine, no more weeping."
No bloody roses, for Cain's wedding."

Beeple was growing impatient. He was thinking that by now, he should have been airbourne. What was wrong? Despite his revitalized power of speech, the Blackbird had not indicated acceptance of the task of transporting him to the Palace of Time. What if Beeple's power of speech left him, like his power of sight had done? Action. Select the words. Voice them. Beeple contemplated.

The bird flew to an almond tree top. The sun was beginning to penetrate the grey clouds. The blackbird began to sing again.
"You are from the tribe of sea
Like the night, you wait on the day
With the hope that you may flee
The Sun's fury before it nestles
in the milky way.
A promise kept, we go to the
Palace of Time
On our way, you may not speak
Or you may have committed your last crime.
Falling out of the transport of my beak.

Hark well my words in this melody
all earth wagers on your oath of secrecy."

The shrill piercing voice of the Blackbird was heard no more. It spread its wings, swooning onto the bamboo that kept Beeple in the hammock, then lifted the contraption with its beak and proceeded to soar skyward with Beeple in the hammock.

Somehow on a broken almond twig which was caught inside the hammock, ocular to the black,gold and white circle of the blackbird, were few orange gold almonds, exuding a pleasant odour. As the flight soared higher and higher, into the haze of the Sun, Beeple felt the increased warmth, as being a signal that his journey would soon be over, he recollected the years before the hammock. His last speech was ready. He would argue on the continuance of Race, Peace, Justice and Mercy. Then a strong compulsion drove Beeple to open his mouth and out of the reservoir of his power of speech, the words blurted.

"What......... is ....your name?" The blackbird grew furious and rabid.

"Black............................!"

The bamboo upright of the hammock jolted. The contraption hurled towards earth.

Beeple gnashing.
The blackbird swooned downwards, past the contraption, retrieving the almond twig with its beak and continued its flight towards the Palace of Time.

Selected Poetry

THE DIAMONDS

For Derek and Roddy Walcott

It have one roof. I not speaking English
When French come easier than de Spanish.
We on we own. You Captain, all of we is crew.
Beginner's luck, safe in harbour, storms brew.
We is one country in chains, we and you
Equal, no master, as in domino and partner.
Simmons syncopated St. Omer's flag; was true
One smaller, twin landmark – yours was bigger.
In this disheveled condition of our confusion
In the lacerated bosom of our constitution
The laboratory for faeces stands on the sea
Picturesque as coral seeds of inconsistency.
Puppets to the whim and fancy of atom and ion
Our currency rare, a one in an even million.
Selling Jalousie National Park for Swiss currency
Is like killing a white elephant for debauchery
Awright nut! No more kings! Charles sings
Calypso while playing golf at de Sulphur Springs.

If my name was Coolie X, I'd sport a complex
Especially as the orchestration of plural sex
Offends my morals, my deeds of sale, lease virility
Old men pause, requisition coitus periodically
Until they look here and there, looking hooker
Line and sinker. Deep sleep. A grave Herr Banker.
For thirty years paid homage to the wiles of a whore
Alongside a jetty where UN sailors built a store
Of arms, legs and breasts of chicken, with a cashier
Domestic servants and a diplomat as town crier.
"Progress is History's dirty joke"...frogs croaking
"Give me a Piton Medal"...my bleeding hands aching
Ignorance breeds arrogance as with de fer de l'Anse
Junior Sec whet appetite for the Common Entrance
I am Pontius Pilate. Omnipotent and considerate
Who dare stand before me naked in locks and gait?
I fine Jacquot, a despotic hero drenched in Calculus
Of Roman industry draconian yet magnanimous.

I forget we is Black skin, white masks of Rodney
Rasputin, Cromwell, Napoleon, Lincoln, Mussolini
Lineage of Victoria, now Boedica, some Helen
Especially at La Rose, every village virgin is Queen.
My tears may not muffle your drums of war. I curse
Those architects of poverty upon my wanton purse
Until the savants perish in the wake of Tutankhamen

Sores rise from your sockets, lost in your playpen.
Destitute like squatters, beggars in our homeland
The Carib artifacts buried beneath the grey sand
The steel of Lancashire's working class indomitable
As the sparse tobacco and fruit surge on our table.
At Morne La Croix, the human sacrifice of a poet
Will not appease Herod's zest for a blood banquet
Dansez Makak. Vieux London. Macbeth in his cell
Now Dante must journey to the bowels of Hell
A crystal ball hovers between the green Pitons
The skymen with the diamond fire claim their lost icons.

****

MORNE DU DON

For Augustin 'Jab' Duplessis
after Luther Francois' compostiton.

I kiss your naked feet
At sunrise when we meet
Across from the street
Where we used to greet
You make my heel
Replace the wheel
And the way I feel
I long to ride steel
Through the concrete
As shacks compete
Footpaths in retreat
Past songs of heat.

Then on either side
of your sinuous slide
in the houses reside
a blushing flush bride
taking photos with pride
protuding political divide
as the voters decide
the results coincide
with another homicide
one unsolved suicide
as ground doves glide
and in palm trees hide.

You dare. Whosoever will
They stare. Climb this hill
You bear. Above the harbour's chill
You there. Calm and tranquil still

Morne Dudon
You hear black and white notes spill

Bare back
Brace back
Morne Dudon

You care for life's cheap thrill?
You bear your brother ill?
You hear who next to kill?
You bear weed from the mill?

Morne Dudon.
En l'heure. Morne Dudon.
En l'heure
Morne Dudon

En l'heure
Yon l'heure Morne Dudon

A l'heure
Morne Dudon.

T'al heure Morne Dudon........

When you beckon night
As the fireflies ignite
The fortress of skylight
I reckon my sight
Is worth its might
In the sea's delight
Of shores in flight
But I trod you light
And plod you tight
Even I would fight
To gain your right
To relieve your plight.

****

MARY WON HER WICK

All of dis and dat happen in nineteen seventy seven...
Drunk from Saturday night's battle with the bottle
They ventured to answer a call of trouble.
On Sunday Babylon went to Morne Gimie
Three thousand feet high, Four hundred years from the naked eye
Where snake, tete chien and Rasta dwell

All afraid of polluted concrete, they preferred Hell.
Summoned to find a watchman's gun
In a forest that could hide a million and one
With a Judas guide, a slave of foolish pride
Marching Babylon on to victory against hungry harmless Rasta enemy.
Babylon come with guns and ammunition
Angered on by their own meaningless condition
And what a find Dollars boggle the mind, borbol
Cultivated marijuana, Babylon take all
Illegal gold, ganja in de soil...
Ras Jomo and daughter Jennifer in cuffs
A fifteen month old baby, all captured by the toffs
Crying for her marijuana tea
Think they would show some sympathy?
Instead hungry Babylon steal from Rasta
Two breadfruit and an orange, maybe dem belly feel a lil strange.
Babylon slept in hell that night, frightful weak heart could no longer fight
Heights sar... lights spar.
Monday before going away
Babi burn out de shacks, bundle ganja into bags unto backs
Why de heavy load down de steep road?
why wasn't it burnt? Up there ? Boy haven't you learnt?
Reinforcements came to applaud the fame.
Dis is mental health week, I have my chance to speak
When mental health week in swing, is only popularity poster thing
Never even mind the price of a white, lil bit of that make you feel alright
Stop issue of liquor license, Boy doan talk such nonsense
Wha goin on in de cuckoo's nest, is not jus one helluva mess
Talk sar walk spar.
Tuesday, the Voice of the Nation publish, a marijuana sensation.
If you doan know what it look like, why not a front page hike
Beaming contented faces void of even animated graces
Telling a story of terror and savagery, a common feature of Babylon supremacy
Then a kindergarten psychiatrist, on de air on this same marijuana business-
He talk of how grass does blow de mind, how it best to leave this thing behind
If you want a high, why not try some whiskey down by me?
I have sixteen brand inna de liquor stand
So why not come, rum make you welcome
Where de mister get so much data
On dis ting that still is research matter?
Sure thing he didn have de right training for what he dere saying
Maybe he ain reading what in de printing
Sight sar fight spar!
Wednesday, early o'clock
With the sound of the morning cock
A pusher's vehicle on wheels
Express sentiment for a crime he feels.
Want to know what this man say on de Radio?

But before ah tell you, let me tell you true, that for St. Lucia is One Love
That is all I know of, but this man show de seeds of dissension
Among de people of de Nation!
He offer reward for hate, that already so rampant in de State
Rasta being victimized by mafia, wick head babi scrutinizing Rasta
War inna de fan club.... War inna de liquor pub.... War inna de family
You never know who is your enemy!
If he think he is a sensation, it's easy to bust his reputation
The price of freedom of action, could place you behind bars in detention
Besides the penalty is always more damaging to the person, than what he's using
But did is a backyard situation, where we unwittingly rape Education -
Doan be no spy for the brotherhood, it's better to be a Robin Hood
Then Firty, say sixty, then eighty
Education Minister sounding sinister, dormant, infant, teacher, preacher, pusher, user!
Which way is easy to say?
How can hungry worried mothers sleep? Education should afford them peace in the deep
The choice of your fate is yours to keep
Free Education, near starvation
Promises of improvement have led to dissent
Just wars have causes!
Think star, ink spar!
Thursday picture change, story re-arrange
Babylon never give up aggravation, so why they try to bluff de nation?
Dem taking care of de situation, look they even want more ammunition
Moreover, now in crime fighting is only Rasta hunting
Gunplay de order of the day -
Why want more, when Rasta cannot handle de score?
Stocking up for de season, which comes with the age of reason.
The power of silence gave Ras Jomo assistance, but they send him to darkened hope
To break him down to cope.
Strength sar, Jah guide spar!
Friday I hear a lil yute ask, she mother for truth
Is what go happen Ma? Everything turn marijuana all of a sudden -
Maybe is a cover up for something, maybe is something they planning!
Dem mind always working.
Clockwork - berserk
You're not indispensable, so be sensible!
Come straight, we settle fate!
But everything is marijuana Ma...President know of it...Mr. Carter Ma?
Yute you like story? Alright in the morning is history!
Some might show objection but it is a seed of revolution
Like freedom is a condition of evolution
De revolution which must come because of that seed, Babylon find troublesome
Yute is your culture that is your future
But where it Rasta? Youth look for it...you find it?
Dem doan give it Rasta..
Heed sar ...Speed spar!
Saturday, time fly fast, today becomes past

Somehow tomorrow becomes now
Back to the Gimie to hunt Rasta enemy.
Soon somebody dead, Police gun fire de lead
All in the course of duty, who's to plead guilty?
Who bears the grudge before Jury and Jah dread Judge?
How many more will die seeing life through Rasta eye?
How long will there be oppression, before the Judgement Day and retribution?

****

INTRANSIT

For Damian 'Sappy' Edwards

Lost and found
One side shoe
Sole gone lace on
All my muddas- heard dis hear dat
All my faddas- all my bruddas - hear dat! Hear dis!
All my sistas know who on de show!?
I go slow! I go fast!
I go know, I go last
Long shot, short shot.
All socks have holes
Me lay day, me day dey
All my matta.
U -we.......u – we
U laff......U laff
U D eye....... U D eye
U car dat on de side dead?
U say R....U say H
U say eye...U say taxi
U kay why !!!!!!!U Say Say
Ku ku klaw kaw ku
Ku on Kaw....ku on Maw
U all o k ?
Santa Kluss wars fuss
Wiff duss vuss Santa
Come in a van....inna transit van
Inna suit
Inna trance. Till death do us
Two part!

I am
In a tomb
I am
In a jam
In a bone
Down town
Corn tree

I am
In a womb
I am
In a room
In a lane
Door clown
Morn spree

Plan in.........plan in...........milk in
I am in human
I am in human
In norm he knee
Bar one

I am
In a man
I am
In a slave
In a love
Dove gown
Born free

I am
In a virgin
I am
In a spin
In a twin
In a diff
Rent sky

Long in longing singing in
Crossing passing
Next one
Kluss klass ku ku laws laws
Crew cook ask 4 U
Look locks click clicks clack
Chief crook put de axle on new!
Driving in a trance sit
Van lil bit on
De side dead!
An out, does shout
An clout, does sprout
An about turn
An inn, does scout
An out
An down, does shout
All about
How he kwhy, kwhy, kwhyet, kwyet!
Why Why
I I
I am in a trance
Sit van lil bit
On de side dead
Oh she in de trance
Sit !?

****

THE GREEN HOUSE

For Earl Bousquet

The Jazz bugs are slowly clawing their minds
Out of the green house while the sea winds,
Lift the skirts of the coconut trees to yield
Dry nuts to fall on the battered battlefield.
Mi Jean Bousquet sauntered on a motorcycle

Ride across the Sans Soucis Bridge, the recycle
Back tyre almost had him on stabilizing stasis.
He'd broken his right leg at the knee cap, scrapes
And bruises, stitches in his right hand. He squeezes
A sponge ball to train the lucidity of the agile grip
That manipulates his vocation of conjuring words
The way two enemies engage their steel swords
Cast in pain on a Victoria Hospital bed conscious
That his wife and family are content to be anxious.

****

LET ME SLEEP

Let me sleep
Dey not letting me sleep
De rats want to sleep with me
De mosquitoes sing in my head
Centipedes stinging me in my eye
The little ply hut have one mash up bed
One bedroom eight children
Man and dog, in and out -
I can hear my neighbour
When she doing her shows
Screaming when she getting her blows
And I doan know dat man dat breed my daughter
And I doan even have a quarter
To make a phone call to my child mother.

Let me sleep
Dey not letting me sleep
All dey have is music
A lot of loud music in de ghetto
And dere ain have no space to
Dance in de ghetto -
Kaan find a work
So I have to sell something
To buy food, clothes
Many, many times on the street
When I couldn't pay rent
I leave Foou Ah Chaux for de Boulevard
Then Conway, now Graveyard
A gun in his hand, my son get mad.

Let me sleep
Dey not letting me sleep
Ah tired see blood, smell vomit, spit
Tired see gunman dying to make it

Ah ain have no bizness of mine to mind
But is my bizness that dey want to mine
Ah tired playing lotto in dis ghetto
Where dere is no hope
Today or tomorrow-
Why can't you and me set
De ghetto people free-
Make all de naked hungry
Children happy-
All dat dey see is misery, poverty,
Angry, dirty
Children crying in the ghetto.

****

CANTICO

For Rosie Etienne

I dance to the rhythm of my soul
While my harp plays the melody.
My eager limbs respond in whole
To the cadence of the symphony.

Sounds pervade the scented air
As I feel my agile body gravitate.
Voluntarily my able legs disappear
My nimble arms just dissipate.

I feel the earth beneath my feet
As the world turns to my heart beat.
My eager head goes into tailspin
Swelling with a feeling from within.

I conga, I samba, I soca, I rhumba,
Cantico I just can't let you go
Cantico I just can't let you go

I bolero, I mambo, I tap, heel and sole

It's all in me so I take control
And let the rhythm of my soul
Carry my weight through a keyhole
On the tip of my appointed toe.

****

The
Difficulties In My
Path Will Not
Defeat My
Ambition

MILLET

For Keith Nicholas

A whole heap of milk
Flowing through the cover
Of a book about silk
Where we then discover

That the teacher was beating
The children with a belt
Whenever caught cheating
That's justice the way he felt.

In his hands he holds
The world's future sky
Today he only cuckolds
To make the children cry.

Far from Mummy's breasts
Upholding the punishment
The verdict vivid now rests
In the arms of government.

The postman rang twice
The TV News was hot
The price of the sacrifice
The cows had no doubt.

****

DEAR TOMAS

For Edge, Sabby and family

By now, you must have heard how your hometown of Soufriere has been brutalized
Tomas transgressed, in a torrent of rain and wind, leaving everyone very traumatized.
Aunty's Home had the roof blown off and there were at the very least twelve deaths.
We have not been able to get all twelve bodies, so we will need less and less wreaths.
I am aware that the grief of this nation, will rise from the depths of pain and sadness
One community has to bear, as the fruits of its labor and due reward, is the madness
We see before our very eyes, our lives assessed, our pride battered, dreams are flung
In the naked navigability of the whirring wind, when none of our verbose voices sang.
We must seek to find the missing persons, with your help and hearts, give them dignity
A resting place to fit, their laudable legacy with a passion pulsating, with deep sincerity
That we, who have witnessed this violent visitation, may lay down our own angry arms
Embrace each other, in fortitude and forgiveness to know our God's merciful charms.

****

ST. LUCIA
Livity Art Studios

YO D

For Billy "Bones" Augustin

You D J
You can
Not hear me
You D B
You can
Not C me
Try B flat E flat
D hat
Walking in
The mourning
Breakfast
C
King the colors
In the thunder
Rain
Bow inside your
Heart
In D sunrise
Clouds and crowds
a four foot flute for
Sabby and family
A shadow in a mirror
A branch of a green bread
Fruit
Butter for a family
Drum La Borde Board
Shack show
Heart attack
Black snow
Billy D. Flower
De Power
Of grass Of Charcoal to Oil
Yo di Jour Ouvert.

****

CLAY

For Catty

Beneath the scorching sun's heat,
As a little girl, you planted your feet
Firmly in the brown bearing earth
Seeing your mother stroke the hearth
Of the heart, where your passion ignited
Into a craft, which you have exhibited

As your calling for this life's survival.
From the early days of your arrival
Along the rivers and ridges of Choiseul,
Where even the stars knew you well
While you shaped utensils, out of clay
Which the needy families used everyday
As was the fashion of sunsets long gone
When your daily battles were to be won.

****

THE MIDNIGHT HOUR

I heard people say they were best of friends, yet this discovery is so scandalous
Shocking, corrupt, reflecting the tip of the iceberg, navigational in the insidious
Which is a sham, a mask for fraudulence, treachery and manipulation of truth
Through utilizing the cunning of serpents, in an amazing war over butter bread.
I never knew acrimony would breed such desperateness as the burden of proof
Just as mosquitoes, become eccentric, in your ears but would prefer you deceased.
Edificial changes based on the eclectic, obscures the ebb and flow of our blood
Their quibble questions about our vision, vests on their conscience in quiescence.
Shuffling between those alphabets, to the sound of drum and acoustic accordion
Architects juggling their daggers like pens, while they open the cage, so the lion
Can have its claws clipped to the cacophony of elephants, monkeys and parrots
Jeering at the spectacle of the transformation from their protected parking lots.

****

DEAF ANNOUNCEMENT

For Matthew George St. Clair 1916-2013

It has been many nights like this one
Listening to my heart's reverberating tone
Thinking of this one great human being
Who took me to his heart's ever living
Showed me compassion and tenderness
In a way my own parents didn't deliver
At any time. The moments we spent together
Remain a treasure in my heart which is
Now failing with disease. Just my guess
Too much fatigue, duress and the stress
Of not seeing you over the last five years
Contemplating how to wipe away my tears
When this moment would come, hypocrites
Would rejoice reviling my heart stopped
But like your elongated breath I have cropped
Another life of poems and songs all my own.

****

GRANT IN AID

For Mikey Smith - Jamaican Dub Poet

Ah we... ah a way.... ah wha you want
Dey grant in aid It's been said..... it's in my head
Ah we.... ah a way
Born inna land behind God bandstand
Beneath the glaze of cardboard and lantern
My godmother was servant to a middle class Master
I was slave ...one freaker fo a Carib.
Come a time when me go Hinglan to walk across London Bridge-
Me didda lime from Trafalgar to Soho, converse inna cockney talk
Till me fix de Deacon fridge. Was Snow White and de Seven Black midasssss
In series on de tee vee in English with kafro kasian sub titles.
For a while was alright, Elephant and Castle had masses of flesh, bricks and honey
Flowed from subway fracases.
Tek me two years to curse, when a dole man tek my purse,
Put it pon a blinking horse de four foot sumpn nuh even place furse.
So u o me, see Romans inna Apple tree
Me, my, and eye, we had to say bye, bye.
Ah we, ah a way, ah wha you want?
Dey grant in aid ...first
When me go a Canada
Me nevah write me sista and brudda. Me left home inna hurry
Cos me didda plan fee marry.
All de street dem was young, de people all didda look strong
Skyscraper and elevator inna one, inna eight lane traffic zone.
Eclectic city of the North, salty tears I miss the green South
Miss my God, acres of Sea and Sunshine, standing frozen inna bus line.
Tee vee running all de time with soap and water committing crime
Mummy a likkle more junk food, woulda make daddy feel real good...
De world's second largest country, wages war on poverty
Was headlines on de Toronto Star but true though they wont get far.
With all dem wealth in dem belt, tink dem feel what me brudda felt
When dem tun him way from de airport
Say im landing papers mek im an illegal import.
Ah we ah a way, ah so dem ah say, dey grant in aid ......second
When time for de USA, me couldn't talk in de yankee way
Still have to eat cold cucumber, any time me get a phone number.
Letters that me pen friends write, all stamps suddenly mean blight.
Is a place with a sense of history, in stone they testify liberty.
Assassination plots and Arlington, jazzination pilots and Washington.
If train nuh go, night nuh come, when you call her tell her your income.
Maybe when you do get to Hollywood, some folk oughta make out you look good
You could get a cowboy costume, go sell the man in the moon perfume.
Was quicksilver and gold reserves of people, peddling what justice deserves.
Green cards whisked in a nuclear plant, in dis ya one, I man mirror ant.
Rushing at the phlegmatic, mutha my sista's now automatic
Was inna flux and fix on a neon trip, some dood bought her a diamond on sunset strip.
Ah we – ah ah way - ah wha you want?

It have a way man tek fraid of de sea and sky man nuh made
Space, tell tale and travel, a black tun white for im navel
Nuh guh nuhwhere else where im born, leave geography to the open door of morn
Him he grants peace of astral, enjoys life's odour continual
In de twilight hours of technology, mission earth is all of anthropology
Ah we, ah a way everywhere we go.........

****

GOD AND COUNTRY

Do you believe in what you preach?
Do you practice what you preach?
Have you got faith in what you're doing?
Have you got power in what you're saying?
Hey brother!
There are those who do it for a show
There are those who say it's right but know
That it ain't the way it ought to be
Although it may not be the only way to go
Being true means saying no
So they close their eyes and don't see
That God and Country should be first in every cause
That God and Country should be the benefactor of our chores.
To your living is there a reason?
To your love is there a season?
In your pause is there a joy?
In your cause is there a goal ahoy?
Watch it!
There are those whom you ought not follow
There are those whose sights are so low
That they can't create their own destiny
Even if some thing shows on the outside from the inside they can't hide
Because truth always conquers vanity.
Live for God and Country, give for God and Country.
Do you criticize, yet say nothing is being done
Instead of thinking of what could have been done?
Do you long to see justice instead of the wrong
That you have suffered from for so long?
Take time
There are those who dictate the way you live
There are those who activate those who give
But take more than enough for one, these hearts are harder than stone
For while others weep and moan, they enjoy the lion's share alone
Still be true to God and Country..... Still have faith in God and Country?

****

NEW WALKING STICK

After all but I got to write this before I retire. At eighty she must be tired.
I got to her house today about ten, yet Auntie was still sleeping as I arrived.
Took her four calls, with me outside the door, for her to open as she
Was very happy to see me, as I was myself to see her in her nightie-
Cos that was pleasing to the eye, as does the aura and feel of the welcome
But I took notice of her reliability, on her new adjustable walking silver stick
While she stood clutching it, almost waltzing with it, as she told me news about home-
Doctor, had charged her, a fast fifty dollars for the swift visit, having dispensed bitter
Wares, a tube of an ointment and maybe twenty pink Ibuprofen tablets.
I joined the fingers of my hands, raising the bond on my head, while I got sick-
She continued to say, that she had not had breakfast but once had a sister
Hence the closed door and the nights have been sleepless with the pain
Induced by a fall, when I was last with her, moments after I had left her
One dark evening, she had grappled with the stubborn inside door and fallen
On her back and head but was able to get up to a new life, dependent to her neck
On her new silver stick, which has become one with her being, as she plods
Through all levels of frustration, a flight of stairs, her sacrifice to our gadabout gods.

www.ingramcontent.com/pod-product-compliance
Lightning Source LLC
Chambersburg PA
CBHW040830050726
47507CB00021B/169
9789768212986